Spectral Evidence

Spectral Evidence

Poems

——◆——

GREGORY PARDLO

Alfred A. Knopf

NEW YORK

2024

THIS IS A BORZOI BOOK
PUBLISHED BY ALFRED A. KNOPF

www.aaknopf.com

Knopf, Borzoi Books, and the colophon are registered trademarks of
Penguin Random House LLC.

Library of Congress Cataloging-in-Publication Data
Names: Pardlo, Gregory, author.
Title: Spectral evidence : poems / Gregory Pardlo.
Description: First edition. | New York : Alfred A. Knopf, 2024. |
Includes bibliographical references.
Identifiers: LCCN 2023003638 (print) | LCCN 2023003639 (ebook) |
ISBN 9781524731786 (hardcover) | ISBN 9781524731793 (ebook)
Subjects: LCGFT: Poetry.
Classification: LCC PS3616.A737 S64 2023 (print) | LCC PS3616.A737 (ebook) |
DDC 811/.6—dc23/eng/20230203
LC record available at https://lccn.loc.gov/2023003638
LC ebook record available at https://lccn.loc.gov/2023003639

Jacket art by øjeRum
Jacket design by John Gall

Manufactured in Canada
First Edition

Dedicated to the memories of Mary Turner,
her husband, Hayes, and their unborn child

Spectral evidence refers to a witness testimony that the accused person's spirit or spectral shape appeared to him/her [the] witness in a dream at the time the accused person's physical body was at another location. It was accepted in the courts during the Salem Witch Trials. The evidence was accepted on the basis that the devil and his minions were powerful enough to send their spirits, or specters, to pure, religious people in order to lead them astray. In spectral evidence, the admission of victims' conjectures is governed only by the limits of their fears and imaginations, whether or not objectively proven facts are forthcoming to justify them. [State v. Dustin, 122 N.H. 544, 551 (N.H. 1982)]. — USLegal.com

Contents

Prologue

The witch mark is sometimes like a blew spot, or a little tate, or reid spots, like flea biting; sometimes also the flesh is sunk in, and hallow, and this is put in secret places, as among the hair of the head, or eyebrows, within the lips, under the arm-pits, and even in the most secret parts of the body.

—REVEREND JOHN BELL, MINISTER OF GLADSMUIR (1705)

Whether the black of the negro resides in the reticular membrane between the skin and scarf-skin, or in the scarf-skin itself; whether it proceeds from the colour of the blood, the colour of the bile, or from that of some other secretion, the difference is fixed in nature, and is as real as if its seat and cause were better known to us.

—THOMAS JEFFERSON, *Notes on the State of Virginia* (1784)

The police officer who shot Michael Brown in 2014 famously described Brown as "a demon" and, although both men were the same height and weight, the officer described Brown's strength relative to his own as that of a professional wrestler to "a rag doll." OK, we get it. He was scared. I don't doubt that he was scared. What I find curious is that an adult criminal justice professional would resort to such cartoonish hyperbole in a court of law to validate his fear and to absolve himself of the irrational behavior his fear inspired. What I find even more curious is that it worked. The court bought it. Not on this one occasion alone. The

"I can't be held responsible for my actions when I encounter a Black guy" defense has worked for longer than any civilized society should care to admit.

To be fair, our lives are haunted. Our language reflects this. We are constantly being stalked and ghosted, both phenomena leaving a paranoiac residue. We are constantly surveilled from eyes cut out of the gilt-framed portraits of men whose names haunt our institutions, their plutocratic legacies endowing certificates and degrees, and the fellowships, scholarships, chairs and charities that our dreams of class mobility ride upon. This book contributes to the work of haunting by searching and researching spectral and physical archives for the ghosts whose presences linger in negative space as the human labor that fuels these vehicles of transformation. Their legacies are no less palpable though often unnamed. My hope is that once we name them, we'll be able to live with them peacefully. Poets are best suited to do this work of naming. Poets are a nation's therapists. And the poets' therapists? Heaven help them.

One of Freud's patients dreamed of "six or seven" white wolves in a tree outside his window. "Wolf Man," as Freud called him, fascinated Freud. Why six *or* seven? Freud wondered, as if his patient should know exactly how many wolves there were in that dream-tree. The uncertainty opened a door that Freud could peep into and find what he wanted to find. Psychosexual trauma, as per usual. I'm not saying he was wrong. Boogeymen in my dreams are similarly sketchy. They are ambiguous and up to no good. I could guess who they are, allowing that they might all be the same person (Dad, is that you?), but I couldn't swear to it. In fact, it's rare that I'd remember any *specific* person—a neighbor, a teacher, or a boss, for example—ever appearing as a villain in my dreams. I realize I'm fortunate in this regard. Many people have tormentors who appear as clearly in their dreams as they do in real life. Me, on the other hand, most often I'd figure out who the evildoer was only after I'd been awake for a while. As if I were interpreting a horoscope or a tarot card, I'd come up with a plausible story to explain the dream and hold someone to blame for my discomfort. But no matter how troubled I felt, I always knew that I was the one who had allowed that person to get under my skin. (Again, I realize this is a privileged perspective and that not everyone can claim dominion so flippantly over the perpetrators of harm in their lives.)

Long before Freud, before the so-called Enlightenment in medieval European and colonial American societies brought an end to the Dark Ages, to be specific, dream interpretation was simple. Everything could be blamed on the devil. Wake up in a cold sweat? That was the devil dragging a chilly finger down your spine while you slept. Dream of wolves in your tree? They weren't wolves, but the devil's minions in wolves' clothing. Even if that did look like your father on horseback in your dream chasing you across the high-school football field cracking a leather belt like a whip over his head while the entire tenth-grade class watched from the bleachers, it was actually the devil. Unfortunately, back then, this also would have meant that your poor benighted father had sold his soul to the devil and, to be on the safe side, you should probably press charges.

Eyewitness testimony is notoriously faulty because it relies on memory, which decays almost immediately. Now imagine testimony based on the memory of a bad dream. Subconscious visions—fear, to put it simply— serving as objective fact. This "spectral evidence" was admissible in court during the Salem witch trials specifically, but in other such trials as well. As I see it, in order to identify the spectral visitor, at least two conditions were likely present. A plaintiff probably had beef with the accused already. Secondly, that beef would have to conform to a prejudice so widely held that the two could coincide within a court of law organically enough as to appear to be reality. Enabled by the state, the accuser in effect becomes the perpetrator by conjuring reality outside the scope of natural law. Spectral evidence is evidence that, technically speaking, does not exist. The magic in witch trials was real. We just attributed it to the wrong parties.

That former Ferguson police officer who fatally shot Michael Brown in 2014 testified in his defense that his fear of Brown justified the shooting. The officer characterized Brown as monstrous: "He looked up at me and had the most intense aggressive face. The only way I can describe it, it looks like a demon, that's how angry he looked." Again, I'm not objecting to the officer's fear. I'm perplexed by the supernatural description. What made the officer so confident that the court would be able to imagine what his demon looked like? What made him confident that the judge and jury would collaboratively map that image onto the person of Michael Brown?

The officer who arrested Sandra Bland testified that he had "observed Miss Bland making numerous furtive movements [in the car], including disappearing from view." Of course, I understand what he means in a colloquial sense. He means that she seemed to have been ducking and hiding from him. But he didn't say that. He accused her of disappearing, as if she were capable of absconding from space and time. We might picture Bland scribbling a spell in the air with a magic wand and vanishing in a cloud of smoke. The officer who shot Laquan McDonald testified that McDonald's "eyes were bugging out, his face was just expressionless," evoking popular images of zombies. Similar testimony from other officers who have used deadly force against Black and brown people armed only with their fearful bodies form an archive of what I argue amounts to spectral evidence.

One of the many poignant insights to be found in Claudia Rankine's 2014 *Citizen* is that Black people are dying "because [the police] can't police their imagination." Like so many social, legal and bureaucratic structures in Western culture, what may seem at first to be an aberration, a flaw in the system, often turns out to be proof that the system is working according to its design. I wanted to challenge our assumption that police *should* police their imaginations. I wanted to question the assumption that policing was ever intended to be objective and devoid of ghosts and specters. Policing was not born out of Enlightenment thinking, but rather out of the medieval belief systems that preceded the Enlightenment. For policing to be effectively forward-looking—that is, for it to be preventative—officers must exercise their sixth sense. Indeed, they are rewarded for their preternatural capacity for probabilistic thinking, that is, their ability to foretell the future. (Think of Axel Foley in *Beverly Hills Cop* in the strip-club scene.) We (the figurative "we") want cops who are street-smart, and who are willing to affirm our beliefs in the criminality of people who "look" like criminals. Police should be able to read a room and identify the criminal the way stockbrokers can sense the ailing stock and sell it short. The connection between policing and capitalism is intentional—the logic is the same. But what would society look like if cops did police their imaginations? Would it be more just or just boring? I think of Elizabeth Warren's comment that "banking should be boring." What if policing were boring? What if cops weren't mythologized as heroes (who nonetheless live in constant fear)? What if we imagined and talked about police officers in the ways that we imagine and talk about schoolteachers?

This book is about the legal means by which fear is used to rationalize the persecution of people imagined to be in league with and possessed of supernatural forces. This book argues that the logic used to rationalize the prosecution of witches is the same logic that rationalizes vigilantism and police street justice. It is the same logic that informs our health-care industry and our educational system. The heart that would slam the brakes on a speeding police van so the prisoner handcuffed in the back would be hurled against the front of the vehicle is the same heart that would use a button installed beneath a desk to lock a door and trap a subordinate coworker inside an office to be sexually assaulted. This book grows out of the provocative if reductive idea that Black men and white women are similarly pressed into service as both muse and monster in the Western cultural imagination. This is reductive because, of course, all women are pressed into such service. Likewise, all men of color have monstrous powers ascribed to them even while they are feminized, infantilized or figured as plot devices in white savior narratives. As a provocation, however, forgiving the binary logic, the social similarities between the violent oppression of Black men and white women at different points in history form an archetypal intersection haunting the mind of Western patriarchy. That ghost, that intersection, omnipresent but rarely named, is Black women.

In the essay "The *Trauerspiel* of the Prostituted Body, or Woman as Allegory of Modernity," Angelika Rauch argues that, in the realm of aesthetics, femininity is a catchall for "the transcendental God, infinity, nature, and beauty." Femininity is not, in other words, "derived from historically extant women, their life context, and their psychological make-up." By examining the lives and experiences of "historically extant women" in their unique singularity, this book examines the impulse to allegorize women. The deadly excesses of frightened police officers, on the one hand, and, on the other, sexual assault by structurally empowered men—these are, as I say, related issues. Why do I care? As an African American male, I have benefited from the unearned privileges of patriarchy, I have internalized its toxic assumptions and I am subject to its daily abuses. This book attempts to survey the damages of patriarchy from the perspective of one who is both its accuser and its perpetrator.

This is a book about my search for evidence, evidence of mental habits that run counter to the values I hope to express in the world. I know these unproductive mental habits exist in me like colonies of bacteria. I won't pretend I can simply eradicate the toxic habits as, following the bacteria analogy, the toxic ones are often symbiotic and interdependent with productive habits of thought. More than a decade of sobriety has taught me that it is impossible for me to change my mind without examining the entire ecosystem of ideas that uphold my worldview. I'm sensitive to the argument that art is not political or that it is not an effective means of political change. Writing, the act of it, has always been the most effective catalyst of change in my life. Every time I want to express a thought or belief, putting it into words and committing those words to some place outside my head forces me to weigh my investment in them. That process changes me, and it changes who I am in the world. That alone moves the needle. I won't call it progress, but it is change.

Spectral Evidence

The Essay on Faith

exordium

While sound and seaworthy, I confess a life of false
confessions, false hearts, ample contempt for bench
warrants charging me with failures to appear.
Let what interest death's elbow grease won't erase
compound, judgments sealed in my ova, my oeuvre,
my juvie, and on Q-tips scribbled like rice grains with
the starshine of my stem cells. Yardsell my cracked
hourglass, my salt-crusted astrolabe, my maps
of the lunar seas. Collect my student IDs, my employee
discounts, my almost-winning scratch-off. Take my voice
mails from the clouds. Dismantle my altar to Walter
Mercado, phrenologist of the stars. But stay memory,
time's plagiarist. Stay poem, spare tire for memory.
Stay reader, beloved, prosthesis for the soul.

narratio

In 18th Century France, Franz Mesmer made friends
dance in synch like iron filings under the magnetized
tips of his Mesmer fingers until further experiments
proved to move the crowd he'd only need his Mesmer eyes.

propositio

From bandshell to boathouse to the shores of Empire Blvd.,
the lindens' scent of fidelity flanked the Botanical's glass womb.
Two cats crooned teakettle falsettos like soul-stirred
buskers swinging a cappella mellowed on a fifth of Thunderbird.
Solo, sneaker soles greased with the ginkgo fruit's perfume,
I found the 9th St. relief of Lafayette at ease, his lowered sword,
the steed and Armistead, enslaved hero spy who, obscured
by horse and history, doubles agency like a nom de plume.
The Marquis adored him, however hapless and off-kiltered
Armistead's depicted. Could they've been lovers? I wondered
under my breath. Could Armistead consent to jump the broom
and camouflage his bondage? In the picture, yet off the record,
he's Lafayette's prisoner no less if Love were his parole board.
Faithful as a terracotta soldier, now he sports a hard rock costume
to picnics and playdates. Who marries a Black man must guard
more than their love, his body taken, in this city's orchard
of bad apples, for sport. Slavery made him a family heirloom,
the booty he was denied. In consolation, he claimed as war-reward
Lafayette's name. His freedom came at the hand of the Lord.

partition

Studies show post-castration a man can experience joy
in his Cyrano, the pet name I imagine clinicians christening
the strap-on. Or Pinocchio. Any of the phallic fables where
the nose denotes a fallacy. Devoid of funk. A rootless longing,
gravity without ground belonging to that appendage existing
like sorry/not sorry, a cartoon limb someone has sawed off
offering support for that person to sit on. I've often mistaken
love for the object of love and been left with a study
in possession. An earlier draft of this poem claimed ecstasy
is muscle memory. I'm of a new mind on this and now feel
ecstasy is a being-beside-myself uncanny as when I've slept
a nerve pinched in my arm and woken to find it's but the warmth
of an egg in a basket of sand long as that storied summer of love,
long as the word that likewise dulls in time to a fist-bump,
periodically needing to clear its cache to regain vitality, to restore
the heft of declaration. So much to unlearn: old selves and my
toxic attachments to them. I pull them from the roll and miss
the perforations. This is life with regret, an infinite regress.
A joyless repetition. A mess of produce bags on the supermarket floor.
I'm clinging to earlier drafts, intimate as chalk outlines, screen
burns, they surface when I hot-breath the mirror. I sit and reflect
on those pronouns wrestled from time and their tether
to a manhood they believed was a part of the body. What joy if
I could only forgive them. If I could love them, if I could just
let them go.

confirmatio

True in the control room at the large hadron collider.
True at a candlelit séance in a Storyville bordello.
A hunger anticipated is no less a hunger, and desire
stayed by whalebone and lace is magnified by the silence
of our Lord. True like the face of an ingénue
embedded in a dowager's demur. True as the miracle
tones chorused from the dwarf star Proxima
Centauri and the whale they call 52 Blue. True
as the judgment of a vengeful mob. Memory foam, wet
concrete outside the high school. Silly Putty takes up
the news: *Ars est celare artem*. True art conceals its artifice,
the longest line crossing the palm of my hand. True the form
thinking assumes that becomes the object of thought.
Mmmmm we say at the TV chef lifting her fork.

confutation

We say "Black bodies" when referring
to the iconography of racism. No one would body

slam a child, but stand your ground against a Black
body and the courtroom says amen. Affirmation

active in the witness's fuzzy memory. The Black
body is no person per se. It is the American

Dream, the via negativa that makes freedom ring. It
is the evidence of things not seen.

digression

Like the ancient Scythians I believe to see is to send spittle-
like rays that grapple an object's cosmic
elements and resemble them in the sweatshop
of the eye a process not unlike tasting with
the nose the hollandaise that surfs a heavy sigh
a measure of telepathy a distance

relation that buckets up from the soul a spitting image
The spirit in the Queen's magic mirror was enslaved there
        Siri tells me   According to Jesus adultery
with the eyes is adultery   Men see says John Berger
As if I need only observe an English muffin
to find its fore-texture printed on my tongue to prove

the tactility of the eye   that lemony emulsion
amusing your bouche, too, sudden jets of saliva
at mention of the lemon-butter's pinch   Don't think of French
kisses   According to seventeenth-century slave
codes imagining your enslaver's death was a crime punishable
by death   I've stopped looking for fear

my looking might hurt someone   by accident,
and I misplace my glasses at the hint
of truths I don't want to see and pat the bench around me
my chest and hips as if I might vanish   Ancient
Scythians blinded prisoners of war to mark them as slaves
A visible distinction   The eyes   The tongue *Mon*
semblable watch me unlock my phone with my face

peroratio

Dear Joni, you've said love is touching
souls. If I reach out to yours now in extromission,
will you register that singularity in the cosmos
of your affection? Will you feel my soul touching
yours just as surely as you've touched mine?

Charm for the Transmigration of the Soul

Christoph Scheiner (1575–1650)
Johannes Kepler (1571–1630)

Thanks to Jesuits like the medieval physicist who
mistook the eyeball for a library of one-page picture
books, each book titled *What I Saw Just Now*, each
book available to the eternal occupant of our mortal
minds and anyone else with a scalpel, we can harken

back to the olden days when chevaliers and musketeers
hunted mature toads for the swampland zen thought
to lodge congealed like caramel candies with sage
and healing properties, in their shovel-shaped skulls.
This charm doesn't need us to believe that our Jesuit,

Christoph Scheiner, hungered for this fabled "toad-
stone" as he groped his way to his discovery through
the double arches in a hopper's head, but he must
have had a reason to dissect the animal when, to his
surprise, something hinted of its picture book, if not

all its lived experience, printed on the tiny bijou
of the frog's eye. God in all things! he must have thought,
astonished. What could be more intimate
or holier than sharing another creature's
vision? This charm derives from Scheiner's science.

Its magick grants us access to other minds the way
a book would, this consummation, its take on the
empathy lacking in dark ages that emerge
whenever books are feared more than guns. Health
food for the mind, this charm works best with

croakers pilfered from biology labs while idle
students graffiti empty shelves in their study
halls. Be mindful of visions that flicker brief as snap
chats as quickness dims and souls escape through
windows of no return. Splay the animals and free

their crystal balls. Appraise these as a thief might:
Pinch them in the light that splinters future into
the faces of kids forbidden reading rainbows.
Repeat the African proverb that says when
an old person dies, a library burns to the ground.

Use this charm to rebuild the bridges that books
otherwise provide. Think of reading as resurrection.
This charm is CPR for lives trapped in histories
stagnating into fable. This charm feeds the hunger
for communion that twinkles every reader's eye.

Occult

Zero your scales to the burden of a lash, Dear
Justice, but let Tituba clumsy the Magistrates'
minds with a wag of her wizened index. A flight
risk near forests of the Wampanoag where Christians
savaged Queen Weetamoo's corpse, what else might
Tituba, nonwhite and woman, haunt but a margin
of error? She's a catbird's song trapped in the chimney.
She's egg whites in water, she is the tumescence
of smoke. Dear Mami Wata, let Tituba prove
to be the stone that splits the stream of their vision.
Let her renounce sight and be unseen. Let her
cough ground coral in the shedding of a pewter
moon, that she, of all the innocents, should live.
Dear Three-headed Hecate, replace her, the unthought
thought, with wax, twigs, horse hair and straw. Let her
not appear as a witness. Nor as evidence. As with
the talking dog, let her be the hoodoo that speaks
through their mirrors. Let a hang-thread skein of yarn
ghost the floorboards tempting a red cat—his familiars,
the devil and his counsel, the canary. Let her conjure
the man in black they fear who charms pilgrims
on the road to paradise, disguised as a harmless
birdwatcher. Dear Nemesis, let her feed the court
a few names from his register—a taste of her
truth, her *mise en abyme*, her one hell that calls forth
another. With no standing on her own behalf,
let her sit in judgment. Let this power
invested of gavel and oath help her give birth
through her mouth like a god.

Question and Answer

Silence padded the aisles
of the auditorium and feathered the many
empty rows expanding between me
and the guy. His voice was a match-
light in the fog until the house-
tech, as if running in ankle-deep snow,
bounded up the aisle with the mic extended
like an Olympic torch for the handoff,
setting ablaze the guy's voice with the question
some of us had already grasped in wisps. "I mean,"
he began again, into the mic, hooking
elbows over the seat back in front of him.
"Do you feel guilty?" he said, more
of a comment than a question.
He was in the shadows. The rest of his class
sat closer, near the stage. "Do you ever feel guilty
exploiting former selves for poems?"
But an earflip had me imagining
my former selves as former slaves.

The present is enslaved to the past, I said, riffing,
not exactly in good faith, to his question.
My voice, a layer of smoke, hung over the seats.
It's the past that runs the plantation.
"I'm sorry," he said, "I zoned for a moment."
He said, "Does this have to be about race? I mean,
it's like," and here he thought deeply
to retrieve his question from the briar patch
I'd cast it into. "It's like your poems are all about you,
but like, maybe your story was never yours to tell."

Know Yourselves

What do you think he meant by that? Was "former selves" a euphemism for something?

I don't know, but the way he put it suggests there's bad business afoot. As if to write poems is to hold lives in the balance, exposing the top-secret archive of one's most precious vulnerabilities.

Maybe that's what they mean in twelve-step lingo when they say you have to take a "fearless inventory" of yourself? Like, you have to inventory all the precious selves you have stored away on the shelves of your moral warehouse.

Don't say it. Please don't—

Self on the shelf.

What if the intrusive thought is the voice of a past self? What if "former self" is another way of saying "imagination," the voice of an awareness that I've trained myself to ignore?

When fascist Italy imprisoned him for thinking out loud in the 1930s, Antonio Gramsci believed everybody should take a self-inventory. He said this was the starting point for developing a critical awareness of the world because history "deposits an infinity of traces" in each of us "without leaving an inventory."

Gramsci did not tell us to write poems about the elusive self on the shelf.

Maybe he meant to be mindful of the inventory. Mindfulness in the dimension of time. You gotta check yourself.

Let's say I buy the fiction that a self can be plucked out of time like a card from a hustler's deck. Why assume that that former self needs protection from the current self? What if my former selves are neither innocent nor helpless? Apparitions, they haunt me from the open graves of people's mouths and try to repossess me, drag me back to their old habits of mind.

The Delphic slogan *gnothi seauton*, "know yourself," I once translated in bubble letters on my middle-school notebook as "master yourself," release the inner tyrant to silence any past-life soul-matter that has been given up to the woods and weeds, forgotten, impossible to locate without that Alice Walker kind of love and bits of dream-sorcery. Pretentious, right?

Am I the only person who thinks self-mockery is punching up?

"Never, I believe," Rousseau confessed, "has any individual of our species possessed less natural vanity than I do."

I've never said *Dear Lord, give me a sign*, but I've often received a sweet nothing as if whispered by one who passed by me in a crowd. Déjà vu, all that. In grade school, I sometimes got textbooks that had answers ghosting the blanks of the chapter tests, and I wondered if my ancestors conspired with my future selves to make school easier for me, either because they thought I was dumb or because they thought I had better things to do with my time.

Sometimes I wonder if my ancestors are speaking through my experiences like vindictive gods sabotaging me for their amusement, inspiring me only to trip me up, lifting me up only to shoot me down.

B.B. King says, "Nobody loves me but my mother, and she could be jivin' too." What if we defined ourselves by our ability to relate to others?

Baldwin writes, "It is to history that we owe our frames of reference, our identities, and our aspirations. And it is with great pain and terror that one begins to realize this [because] one enters into battle with that historical creation, Oneself, and attempts to re-create oneself according to a principle more humane and more liberating."

Let's say progress is a practice of imagining a web of relations that is more empowering than I believe it to be at present. Then to "make progress" is to rethink the stories I tell myself about myself. And to tell my story, I would have to reorient myself in relation to the stories of others.

In other words, my story is not mine to tell.

OK, I'm convinced. My imagination is a spare self that exists outside of time. It's my "already-there-and-doing-it" self. It is my spectral caddie, my familiar, my Magical Negro, my "Man Friday."

Vacuum domicilium. Lights on, no one home. I think, yes, zombie movies are movies about categories of people whose interior lives, by virtue of their social category, are beyond my ability to imagine. Whenever I look at someone on the subway, say, and consciously or unconsciously acknowledge that that person has a capacity for self-awareness, I immediately feel more at ease in their presence.

Zombies. America is afraid of zombies. And labor unions. Modern slavery created zombies by terrorizing people into believing—or at least pretending to believe—that they lacked self-awareness. This took a lot of terror. Like, think of the amount of love it takes to make someone *believe* you love them unconditionally, and replace that love with terror.

Had to be exhausting terrorizing people 24/7. It's why Americans need guns. We're terrified of the ghosts we've inherited.

Maybe the inventors of race thought they could create happy zombies, benign extensions of their own imaginations, their already-there selves whose cultures, bodies and minds lay waiting to be made useful. Problem is, they couldn't entirely convince themselves that their zombies lacked self-awareness. Deep down, they always knew they were just hurting people.

Artistic ambition, for me, means to imagine what my wiser future self might have created and left behind—a manuscript in the dusty synapses webbing the attic of my mind—that I might discover and claim as my own. The future is a plagiarized memoir.

Do I feel guilty exploiting future selves for poems?

Before he asked his question, I was explaining to his classmate how I write to trace the progress of my character based on the evidence of past behavior, to dispense with judgment, whatever comes after forgiveness, neither buoyed by pride nor distracted by shame.

I don't think this was done consciously, but the student was trying to prevent me from using my own experience as evidence for the conclusions I draw about the world.

"Know yourself" could also mean that we should know our place in society, stay in our lane, so to speak. Forsake all ambition. Surrender self to context and disregard history.

A friend says it means we should be aware of impulses that scuttle our prayers. The mind is a horse ridden by a monkey, she says. In Vodou, the body is a horse ridden by spirits human and divine. In Christianity, the soul can be likened to a horse ridden by the devil. Before the invention of the subconscious, there were demons. We were held by otherworldly smokes bent on using us as instruments of chaos. Women and Blacks, as it was popularly thought, were especially vulnerable to such possession.

How can a nation heal if it believes its story is not its own to tell?

[Sonnet]

Racial bias in pain assessment
Kelly M. Hoffman, Sophie Trawalter, Jordan R. Axt, M. Norman Oliver
Proceedings of the National Academy of Sciences Apr 2016, 113 (16) 4296–4301; DOI: 10.1073/pnas.1516047113

"Study 1" documents beliefs of white laypersons
"Study 2" documents beliefs of white medical students and residents

Table 1. Percentage of white participants endorsing beliefs about biological differences between blacks and whites

Item	Study 1: Online sample (n = 92)	Study 2			
		First years (n = 63)	Second years (n = 72)	Third years (n = 59)	Residents (n = 28)
Blacks age more slowly than whites	23	21	28	12	14
Blacks' nerve endings are less sensitive than whites'	20	8	14	0	4
Black people's blood coagulates more quickly than whites'	39	29	17	3	4
Whites have larger brains than blacks	12	2	1	0	0
Whites are less susceptible to heart disease than blacks*	43	63	83	66	50
Blacks are less likely to contract spinal cord diseases*	42	46	67	56	57
Whites have a better sense of hearing compared with blacks	10	3	7	0	0
Blacks' skin is thicker than whites'	58	40	42	22	25
Blacks have denser, stronger bones than whites*	39	25	78	41	29
Blacks have a more sensitive sense of smell than whites	20	10	18	3	7
Whites have a more efficient respiratory system than blacks	16	8	3	2	4
Black couples are significantly more fertile than white couples	17	10	15	2	7
Whites are less likely to have a stroke than blacks*	29	49	63	44	46
Blacks are better at detecting movement than whites	18	14	15	5	11
Blacks have stronger immune systems than whites	14	21	15	3	4
False beliefs composite (11 items), mean (SD)	22.43 (22.93)	14.86 (19.48)	15.91 (19.34)	4.78 (9.89)	7.14 (14.50)
Range	0–100	0–81.82	0–90.91	0–54.55	0–63.64
Combined mean (SD) (medical sample only)		11.55 (17.38)			

For ease of presentation, we shortened the items; see *SI Text* for full items and additional information. For ease of interpretation and ease of presentation, we collapsed the scale and coded responses marked as possibly, probably, or definitely untrue as 0 and possibly, probably, or definitely true, as 1, resulting in percentages of individuals who endorsed each item. Bold entries represent the items included in the false beliefs about biological differences between blacks and whites composite.
*Items that are factual or true.

Nunsploitation

Teresa Ávila buzzes me in then makes me leave
my shoes in the foyer before I enter the Upper East Side
tabernacle of shame she calls a "therapist's office" where
she divines the truths disguised by my confessions.
As my bare feet cross the cold parquet, dark and cloven
to a sticky rhythm, Teresa asks if I'm still tempting the goat
paths that rim the ravine my passions trickle into. It's true,
I'm in love with my therapist. Blame the saint's books
that harken from half a millennium away. I love her unattainable
intimacy, her use of my inner ear to give goose
bumps on the brain. The voice that is and is not Teresa's channels
canticles and conjures woodcut illustrations of my beloved
sprouting poems from her desk at Valladolid, above her a dove-
thought winging through numinous yonder break. Teresa and
Teresa and Teresa in concert fanning out in imitation of a Hindu
god. You'd expect compassion from someone who gentled
her mind inside seven mansions of prayer while feeding
flames her love letters to keep them from prying eyes. Instead,
she saint-splains the dangers of transference as if I never noticed
my itch to project the idea of one thing onto the figure of another,
as if professing love to my therapist meant only to mask mommy
issues. And anyways, isn't that a bit sanctimonious coming from
someone saving her love for a father figure whose image reflects
the sum of all creation? A love so consuming her inside song
reached the sistren's ears glued to her office door, song quoting
an erotic élan, a harmony of relation probing the mystery of self-love,
which is, of course, where love begins. Ipso facto, love is nothing
but transference. Love is squeezing people's feet into
fetishes we've schlepped hill and vale, since memory, like moon-
light, was the surplus of a previous life. To have come this far,
across the park through ramble and glade, knowing the glass
slipper would fit almost any ol' foot I put in it—let the bean-counters

of love call that transference. Let them name this affliction what
they will as if diagnosis were a cure. Let them tabulate salvation,
tell me how many hair shirts and unanswered
hungers. Tell me how many shoeless steps to beatitude.

Allegory

Professional wrestler Owen Hart embodied his own
omen when he battled gravity from rafters to canvas

in a Kansas City stadium. Like a great tent collapsing,
he fell without warning, no hoverboard, no humming-

bird's finesse for the illusion of flight, no suspension
of disbelief to hammock his burden—the birth of virtue—

in its virtual reality. His angelic entrance eclipsed
when his safety harness failed. He fell out of the ersatz

like a waxwing duped by infinities conjured in a squeegee's
mirage. Spectators wilted as the creature of grief emerged

to graze on their sapling gasps and shrieks. I'd like to think
that, freed of self-hype, he realized his mask was not a shield,

and that he didn't spend his last attempting to method
Zeno's proofs. EMTs like evangelicals huddled to jolt

the hub of Hart's radiating soul as fans prayed the stunt
might yet parade the emperor's threads wrestlers call *kayfabe.*

Kayfabe, a dialect of pig Latin, lingo for the promise to drop
at the laying-on of hands. To take myth as history. Semblance

as creed. A grift so convincing one might easily believe
it could work without someone else pulling the strings.

Epistemology of the Phone Booth

I found the scrap of *City Paper*
classified, the 1-900 number and photos
like candidates there, in love's voting machine.

*Dis*comfort station. No pissoir. Hothouse maybe for
a fourteenth-year sprig: me. Light box
to slideshow the introvert
      cloaked in a prepaid identity

discreet as a shirttail in the fly.
                    Ma Bell's shelter
was brutal & snug. I'd heard the ram's horn hum.
A hymn. Just like prayer I thought. No answer.
Clack'd the splendid tongue
                and bloom!
Salutations rose like pollen, prepped me for
      the inverse of police
sketch artists, the one who would evoke so I could render,
in my mind, the enigma of the wanted; one to source
      the vacuum wrenching stutters like rivets

off my tongue.
      Plink. Into the sewer of the mouthpiece.
Then the universal ballad of the waiting room.
Casiotone.
            Hold (me) music.

          No orgone
closet. More like that other-lonely doom—the body
encapsulated, its inventory ever unknown.   Dantean vestibule.
Anti-chat room.
         When the genderless voice beyond
began to lavish I grew ears all over,

                   inner ears
swiveling from one tepid libretto to the next
tuning for some satin frequency the culture
promised until, I repent (forgive me father), the card went bust.

Theater Selfie

Every seat from heaven
to the mezzanine envied ours, seventh row

orchestra, leash-limit of the real.   *#blessed*
#livingthedream   Smug-polite, we shouldered down

the aisles choked with tourists busy puppy-
sneezing their cell phone cameras mostly at

themselves. Because our tickets were a Christmas solid,
house seats at eighty bucks apiece, I hoped to dodge

whichever goddess taketh away from those who make
parade floats of their fortunes, and kept my selfie

game turned low, just a shot of our thumbs: mine dingy-
nailed and elephant-skinned, the kid's kid-sized and

glossy as the ticket stubs and *Playbill* we held
like proof of life against the backdrop of the stage.

Meanwhile, a voice—perhaps the goddess from the
machine—declared all photos were forbidden, which

made me think of footage smuggled from the tender-
age cages of McAllen, Texas, and made me fear our

souvenir selfie might be frisked from my phone by
jackbooted ushers, and the photo's faceless humility

proven moot in the lineup of a falsely modest feed
replete with my bathroom body cropped headless

as a saint or with the phone shielding my face like
a misplaced fig leaf. My friends' tattoo selfies

with their cellophaned frames of skin pigmented
like storefront church windows, faceless, but doubly

begging for breaking on the wheel or whatever
punishment suits the sin of branding oneself

to make oneself a brand. One of many reasons
one should never send unbidden photos of man-junk—

they fail to fascinate in the way the phallic
amulet Romans called *fascinus* might, worn to ward

off *invidia*, aka the Evil Eye, but they do invite
the curse that wipes the member from the body

politic. There is no hiding from the closed-circuit
karma obscura. Which might be reason enough

to unburden ourselves of all things hidden,
to make our lives transparent as a middle-schooler's

backpack. I like to think I gave my kids—even as
their profiles etched in clouds, their data

pollen-green and fossiled onto motherboards,
even as the future makes the past impossible to escape—

blank slates on which they could imagine selves
the world has never seen, but the values we

christen them with are subliminal trackers meant
to keep them homing to their first fold and assuage the fears

their mom and I hold of that proverbial white van—
dope-dealing ice cream man, the predatorial piper whose

domestic terrors are fought with thoughts and prayers.
How can I teach them to live with joy, their hearts

unshuttered and vulnerable when, as I admired
each in turn their God-kissed newness cupped

like chicks in the car-carriers home from the hospital,
I considered spitting in their faces as one neighbor insisted

in her native brogue a parent must do with a child
that is too beautiful—early humiliation preempting

future envy—for her own good? Is it possible a neighbor
could love my kids as if they were hers while I disguise

my fear as care, and hope my silence inoculates them
against jealous gods, hope my absence from the selfie will

exempt them from the crappy roles I've had to play
in this American caste, that fear masking a more primal one

that I can't spiritually afford these tickets and am
unworthy of their love? For what could I do but fear when

life's theater is full of ghosts and mirrors and baleful
peacock feathers? How do I not make worthiness

the measure? How do I prevent my specters
and dreams of childhood from upstaging the child?

Tall Poppies

Rwandan State radio said *cut down*
the tall trees. Listeners heard kill
your Tutsi neighbor.

Dog whistles, dangerous as poetry.
When someone says something like
Trees that grow taller

than the forest will be trimmed by the gale,
they are offering the terms
of your surrender.

500s, BCE, Tarquin the Proud
found his boy busy playing
tee-ball with seed heads

where their garden grew the tallest poppies,
and taught him that, one day he'd
have to lop the heads

of men from whose seed insurrection might
flower. Jump cut, poppies flush
London Tower's moat

ruddy in remembrance of England's blood
shed since the Opium Wars
when Brits by lethal

persuasion peddled addiction for all
the tea in China. *The drug*
to start with and stay

with, Purdue Pharma called OxyContin,
at once slogan and decree.
The bitter end of

palliative care assured as millions
like my dad lined up to meet
their makers thumbing

morphine drips like jumpy kids with click-pens.
'Merican justice hums *kill*
them before they grow,

and poisons the terroir of voting wards,
school boards and precincts, and treats
blooms as invasive

products of graft. Playing like suburban
dads, Israeli colonels claim
they're "mowing the lawn."

Erasure

ing. You better go back to your law books.'' The most
accomplished housemaid, maid-of-all-work, laundress, nurse,
dining-room servant, in our household was a woman named
Emily, and the most accomplished man-of-all-work, carpen-
ter, coachman, 'possum-hunter, fisherman, story-teller, boy
amuser, was Emily's brother, Andrew. They had been
given to my father in his youth by my grandfather, and had
attended him to college, working in the dining-room, to pay
for his education. They were present at my father's wed-
ding, and for twenty years remained members of the house-
hold, exceedingly useful and skilful ; and, I may add, ex-
ceedingly privileged characters. They far surpassed in
efficiency and versatility any white laborers in the county.
I remember, one Sunday, the family came home earlier than
usual from church, there being no services on account of the
illness of the minister. On entering his bed room my
father beheld a strange and yet familiar looking Negro
arrayed in dress-suit standing in front of the mirror, with
arms akimbo, and swallow-tails of the coat switching from
side to side in token of pride and satisfaction. It was
Emily, arrayed in her master's best suit, enjoying a new
sensation. No punishment was inflicted on her. Nor do I
remember that any of my father's slaves were ever punished,
except such switching as was given the children, on which
occasions I was usually present, a most unwilling partici-
pant and fellow-victim.

When emancipation came at the close of the Civil War, it
was understood by the average Negro to mean freedom from
labor. Freedom, leisure, idleness was now his greatest
pleasure. How delightful it was to tell old master now that
he had business in town and couldn't work to-day ; to leave
the plow and hoe idle ; to meet other Negroes on the streets,
to spend the day loafing, chatting, shouting, oftentimes
drinking and dancing or quarreling and fighting. Sambo
was now a gentleman of leisure, and he enjoyed it to the
full. It was easy to live in the South. The mild climate

Supernatural Bread

Lexington Avenue tugged the bus to Easthampton
like a joke dollar bill just out of reach each time
I neared it having missed its stop at 77th, and chased

it to the next which I hoped would be 69th but had to bet
on 66th when the curtain of traffic drew back to show
its brake lights squint, a wounded beast retreating,

but I gave chase as if myself pursued by zombified regrets
hot on my heels, nostalgic for my undoing, though it wouldn't,
the bus, in fact stop until it reached the curb at 59th,

after I'd slalomed bodies under the Hunter College
jet bridge, got beyond the aromatic reach of halal
carts and the Greek grill truck, caterers to immigrants'

catalyst of class mobility, as a mist slicked
my rucksack plus the duffel I had packed because
there is no night bus back to Manhattan, and I'd had

to stay the night out there where it was more like New
England than New York, but every border is a false
horizon, a dream of the Red Sea's righteous

discretion. In Easthampton I roomed in an eighteenth-
century farmhouse the restoration of which
was overseen by this owner-guy who bad-mouthed

universities as hotbeds of treason, professors
consumed by hatreds that have no source, but I was
probably okay, he allowed, as a poet, that is, someone

whose art is impartial and should, he said, like a good
education, make nothing happen. He talked of
sovereignty and his frustrations with "landmarking"

—the illusion that one's environment can be arrested
in time to appoint the land as a shared ancestor,
its immortal aura enameled by the law, but his complaint

outlined the injustice that laws could limit his use
of his property based on "rumors," as he called them,
the unrecorded oral record, that the farmhouse once

harbored fugitives, you know, from before the Civil War,
he said, gesturing to antiquity, time beyond
memorial, and I saw them, haunting, forever tied

to this place, and I thought to ask him why euphemize
slavery as if uttering the word might revive a statute
of limitations like a covenant on the land we occupied.

Haven't we progressed? His question rattles the Great
Chain of Being, its eugenic agenda and the botched
ontology it describes, but I held my tongue and harbored

in my head the weary travelers chasing liberation which
by nature has to lurch just out of reach each time it gets
precipitously close to revealing itself as the mere

abstraction that it is, the way even the harbor
in my mind reduced the fugitives' lives to an allegory
of my own as if we'd together received all tomorrow's

blessings in catching the coach that moseyed down Lex—
as if, indeed, the very pachyderm of time itself would
have left a bus-shaped door in the rain, the threshold

of the future neither coming into view nor losing focus,
the living thread of our connection being the divine
imagination that runs among and through us without end.

Nunsploitation

But for that "iron's point" blushing, O Lord,
like a cautery tool for the wounded soul, the marble and
bronze idles, an engine of reverence and tourism
Bernini distills as "ecstasy." This concupiscence, this
tantric sneeze. Could Bernini have rendered a pleasure,
Lord, not got at the end of a spear? The "Highest Angel"
haunted Teresa Ávila like a Motown hook and prodded
her body quiverish with love's heart-burner, a rapture
fantasy fathomed by her innermost yoga, her spirit
burst forth, O Lord, like a jelly jar full of lightning
bugs clumsied from my handlebars. Beneath the hoody,
her head lolls sweetly with the funk of that agony
glorioso which, if you don't know, now you do
because Bernini lifted Teresa's story, Lord, like a shipwreck
from its ecclesiastical groove and mimicked her signature
miracle, levitation, which she murmured into her sack-
cloth and wimple. He left Teresa's left
foot exposed as if to bait—a bedside tidbit—the devil for
whom she had no fear for he appeared to her toy-sized
and black, and dropped by to make her pound air with laughter,
all weightless, all risen by pinch and tickle until she wet
him with holy water. Lord, tell me that empathy
like art is useless and necessary, that Bernini's inspiration is
more than a contact high. Whatever he named it, Lord,
this bone-still cinema, this spartan delight, forgive him.
Forgive us all, Lord, we lesser creators who conflate
our subjects' demons with our own.

In the Name of the Mother

What was it about this group—which never numbered more
than a few dozen—that inspired the US government, at all
three levels, to spend hundreds of thousands of man hours, and
millions of dollars, working toward its destruction?

—RICHARD KENT EVANS

Homeschoolers, raw vegan zero-wasters, back-to-Nature
nurturers, they moved against puppy mills
and flop houses, against zoos and the avarice that fuels
The System. Responding to a noise complaint in '76,
police subdued the Africas of MOVE with clubs, nightsticks.
An infant, Life Africa, was crushed under an officer's boot.
He'd been delivered at home, and the Commonwealth would
neither certify the birth of Life after death, nor the tears
of a mother named Africa. MOVE kept moving each time,

like a river, their movement was dammed by police, an agency
shamed for its failure to contain them. In '78, a riot-geared blue wall
encircled the creaky Victorian, MOVE's headquarters, while canvas
hoses fed into cellar windows where the Africas held strong,
and forced them to swim for safety.
Deluge upon deluge. Water, bullets. An officer shot from behind
in the melee sparked no investigation. Instead, the city erased
the vacated house as if it were a bit of graffiti, and announced—a social
execution—MOVE were now cop-killers.

Those Africas not given life
sentences repaired here to this tidy block of mother-loved
homes on a street named to honor the Osage Nation. Here,
where MOVE took its last stand, and let the living stray

indoors and out, the compound was a hive the city clawed at
and swatted, passions fermenting like compost.

John Africa, before becoming "Body F," the sixth of eleven bags of
     charred
remains sent to the morgue, wrapped MOVE in the manifesto
they megaphoned all hours ("you can't describe something profane
without using profanity"), and drowned out the music of ice cream trucks.

               Until Mother's Day of '85. Police went door to door
to door instructing moms to pack their families into overnight bags.
Without so much as their arms could carry, they left behind Bibles
and tax records, record collections and Commodore 64s. They left
     bowling
trophies, wedding knives and archives of *Jet* magazine, family albums
and photos propped on credenzas and on top of their Magnavox TVs.
They left wall-hung pictures of King, Kennedy and Jesus when, stopping
to gossip and speculate, they filled the street that'd been cleared as if
for a block party. In 24 hours, they'd watch the city deliver its gift.
The Commissioner's recipe for eviction: M-16s, Uzi submachine guns,
sniper rifles, tear gas, approximately ten thousand rounds of .50 caliber
bullets, more than 500 officers, 640,000 gallons of water and one State
     Police
helicopter to drop 2 lbs. of mining explosives combined with 2 lbs. of C-4
on the MOVE family compound's roof.

As flames rose like orchids in a vase, the canvas hoses parched
and let an infernal peace engulf the neighborhood. By sunrise, whole
blocks lay open like egg cartons, buildings reduced to their earth-
works, sirens sounded their jubilee to match the mothers' wailing.
Timbers in rubble like mulch piles smoldered as smoke left shadows
espaliered on walls, and twined staircases aimed at the unblemished sky.

Notes on Ch. 3

1. "Facial angles" is a reference to Buffon and Camper.
2. See Gall's 27 bumps on the head.
3. cf. Nott and Gliddon's *Types of Mankind.*
4. cf. Semonides's "Types of Women."
5. cf. Myers-Briggs.
6. "She's a six," qtd. variously in undated White House meeting notes, 2018.
7. See Charles Fourier's 1816 satire *The Hierarchies of Cuckoldry and Bankruptcy* detailing forty-nine types across three classes.
8. Market price.
9. Madison Grant, conservationist and hunting partner of Theodore Roosevelt, was instrumental in efforts to secure the 1906 exhibition of twenty-three-year-old Ota Benga in the Monkey House of the Bronx Zoo.
10. The Linnaean Society writes, "Having placed humans within the animal kingdom, Linnaeus distinguished them from other animals in the same order of Anthropomorpha by the ability to 'know thyself' ('Nosce te ipsum'). This would lead Linnaeus to attribute the specific epithet *sapiens* to the genus *Homo* when he began to use his binomial nomenclature in the 1750s. He then proceeded to classify humans further."
11. *Ozawa v. United States* (1922).
12. Or what Fourier calls *hierarchies,* suggesting classification is an expression of power.
13. More simply put, see Marcel Mauss: "those who squat and those who sit."
14. Refer to De La Chambre's physiognomy.
15. Extrapolated fragment from Hesiod's catalog of women.
16. Specifically, I have in mind the asymmetry between Charlie's and Milton's angels.
17. Collected in the "Book of Wikked Wyves" referenced by the Wife of Bath's fifth husband, Jankyn.

18. This is according to an unverified exchange between Edward Curtis and Jacob Riis. James Van Der Zee's response is not mentioned.
19. Linnaeus includes a race of monsters. The Blumenbach, sadly, does not.

Theater Selfie

Ginger, forty-something Latina, wears a flowy linen smock. She is Sara and Fita's mom, married to Greg.

Ms. Cato, social worker. Late thirties, stern; slightly asthmatic; West Indian–American with a vague (not Jamaican) Caribbean accent; wears a purse slung across her chest, shoulder to opposite hip. She carries a bright pink Hello Kitty spiral notebook rolled into a tube.

Greg, forty-something, African American, tennis-player-fit (as opposed to gym-fit), wears suburban Alpha-dad jeans, white oxford shirt and boat sneakers. Sara and Fita's father, married to Ginger.

Elena, social worker. Late twenties, New York ethnic white (Middle Eastern or Eastern European); sometime grad student. She is dressed accordingly.

Fita, approximately eight years old.

SCENE—Parlor of a Brooklyn brownstone. The house is eclectic with bric-a-brac and souvenirs from years of travel. Shelving on the exposed-brick wall stage left is overstuffed floor to ceiling with books. A leather sofa lines the wall downstage right. Upstage right, pocket doors open to a small hallway, vestibule and stairs. Sunlight from the windows upstage paints the parquet floor in grids. In the center of the room is a harp, stool and music stand. Nearby, Ginger sits in a Victorian wingback paired with a Danish-design rocking chair. Both are opposite the sofa and centered on a vintage factory rail-cart that serves as a coffee table. The two social workers from Child Protective Services occupy the sofa. While Ms. Cato and Ginger talk, Elena surveys the room from her seat.

GINGER: You didn't have to come all this way. I can tell you exactly where this is coming from.

MS. CATO: Where what is coming from?

GINGER: The woman who owns the house next door. She's the one who called, right?

MS. CATO: Reports are anonymous, miss. I'm sorry. We're only here to confirm the well-being of the children. Are they at home? Can we see them?

GINGER: [Laughing] I'm afraid that's not happening. Quite frankly, you're lucky I let you in my door. You think I'm letting you near my kids? [Uncomfortable pause. We hear the muffled sound of a crying infant.] That woman lied to get back at me for reporting her to the DOB.

MS. CATO: [Covertly reaching into her bag to silence her phone] Miss, Child Protective Services is entirely separate from the Department of Buildings.

GREG: [Entering] Yet both agencies tell people what they can do within the walls of their home. I mean, this is surreal. It's as if we're being doxxed or something. No, this is way worse. Who would threaten their neighbor's kids?

MS. CATO: [To Ginger] This is Mr. Pardlo?

GREG: Mr. Pardlo is my father. You can call me Greg.

MS. CATO: Good afternoon, sir. I was about to ask Mrs. Pardlo if you often fight with your neighbors.

Surprised, Ginger glares at Cato.

GREG: Maybe I can clear this up for you ladies. Birkenstock Barbie over there had a full-on construction crew practically gut-renovating her house with nary a permit in sight.

ELENA: [Not entirely under her breath] "Birkenstock Barbie"?

GREG: We could tell she was trying to put in a new bathroom on the parlor floor because her guys broke through the party wall like the Kool-Aid Man. I should probably explain what a party wall is. See, there are three layers of brick between each house—

MS. CATO: Ma'am, would you say you and your husband have frequent conflicts?

GREG: Us? Hah, of course! What married couple doesn't?

MS. CATO: [Still speaking to Ginger] In other words, would you say there is tension in your home life?

GREG: I mean, we have ups and downs like everybody, sure. [Looks to Ginger for agreement]

Cato makes notes in the Hello Kitty notebook.

MS. CATO: Have you ever lost your temper with the children?

Together.

GINGER: No.

GREG: Who hasn't?

MS. CATO: Mr. Pardlo, could you describe a time when you've lost your temper?

GREG: Off the top of my head? Well, there was the time I took the girls and my niece to the Met. The opera, not the museum. Lincoln Center. I like to do that kind of thing, take them to places where the world will try to tell them they don't belong. Sara, my older daughter, had an attitude all day for some reason. As we were walking out, she said something that set me off, which in hindsight was probably her plan. But it wasn't just that. I don't remember what she said, but she said it just as this older white lady was walking by us, and the lady had started to give me that smile, you know? The smile that says, *It's so sweet to see you breaking the stereotypes of Black fathers.* It reminds me of this line in a Dave Eggers book where he says something about how seeing Black men with babies makes him smile. Like I'm a dog on a skateboard or something. I mean, I admit I was wrong to snap at Sara. I apologized immediately.

GINGER: Please. [Raises her hand as if to silence him]

Ms. Cato continues writing.

GINGER: [Smiling] He takes them to the opera. He takes them to the theater. He takes them to the US Open . . . You get it.

MS. CATO: Super Dad, huh?

GINGER: Pffft! I guess. He can do that because I do the less-fun stuff. I

45

make sure they practice their instruments. I get them to school on time. I arrange their playdates.

We hear the crying infant ringtone again.

GREG: When's the last time they went on a playdate?

GINGER: I organize their birthday parties.

GREG: Sweetie, they haven't had a party since they were toddlers.

GINGER: "Mr. Pardlo" here could help with the grocery shopping once in a while. And still they expect me to clean up after them. All of them.

ELENA: No, I get it. It's nice that there's a fun parent, but somebody has to keep the ship on course.

GINGER: You know?!?

ELENA: Listen, I know this is uncomfortable, but we need to inspect your refrigerator and your cupboards. Is the kitchen downstairs?

GINGER: Of course, whatever we need to get through this.

GREG: What happened to not dignifying these accusations?

MS. CATO: [Silencing her phone] And we need to see the girls' room.

GREG: You mean rooms. They each have their own room. This is a big house. You see this house? This is a big house. We bought this house practically with jars full of nickels and dimes at a time when all of these neighbors would have been too scared to walk down our block.

ELENA: It must have been hard for you carrying all of those jars to the bank. You want to show me your smoke alarms?

GREG: Have we met?

ELENA: Miss, maybe you can show Ms. Cato downstairs and Mr. Pardlo can show me the girls' rooms? [Elena looks to Cato for approval.]

GREG: Make sure you show her the backyard.

GINGER: I think Fita's downstairs. [Shouts] Fita!

Ginger and Cato exit.

MS. CATO: [Offstage] OK, but, just to inform you, we need to speak to the children alone.

Sound of feet on stairs, voices growing faint.

GREG: Isn't that against the law? Doesn't she need our permission to speak to the children?

ELENA: She'll probably ask—to be polite, but she doesn't need permission to speak to the children.

GREG: You're wasting your time, you know.

ELENA: [Standing] Maybe, but we still have a job to do. [Begins looking around the room, scanning the bookshelves] You're a writer, right?

GREG: You know my work?

ELENA: No.

GREG: Oh. I guess it's obvious. [He gestures toward the bookshelf and pauses before he lifts a picture frame from the shelf.] We were in Honduras that summer. I rented a beach house to work on my second book. Ginger and the girls came down to visit.

ELENA: I don't know any of these books.

GREG: I'll bet you know John Locke. [Pointing] He compared children to idiots—"an idiot scribbling on a blank slate"—because they didn't make proper use of their minds and left them uncultivated. He also thought Native Americans had no claim to their land because they didn't farm or build on it.

ELENA: [Pulling a book from the shelf] Hmm. Yeah, I recognized you when we came in.

GREG: But you said you don't know my work.

ELENA: A.A. meeting.

GREG: Huh. Which one?

ELENA: Brooklyn Heights. The big one. I don't share very often. Not as often as you share. And share. [Beat] And share.

GREG: I knew you looked familiar! Wait, isn't this some kind of conflict of interest or, I don't know what you want to call it, privileged information?

ELENA: At the meeting, you told a different version of the Lincoln Center story. I notice you left out the part about going all Alec Baldwin on your daughter and screaming at her in front of the "rich white folks" by the fountain.

GREG: I mean, shouldn't you have recused yourself or something when you recognized me?

ELENA: You must spend a lot of time polishing your stories.

GREG: What does that mean?

ELENA: At one meeting, you got really worked up about people in Denmark speaking English to you when you were trying to learn Dutch.

GREG: Danish.

ELENA: Danish. Danish? Danish. Said you'd start speaking Danish and they'd hear you fishing for words and right away they'd switch to English. You compared that to people not respecting that you were in recovery and trying to get you to be the party guy. It was weird. You were so frustrated that I guessed you must have been spoiled as a kid. Where else would you get the idea that people should see you as you want to be seen? No one has to participate in your self-image.

GREG: [Chuckling] That's right. You were the timekeeper. The enforcer. Now it all makes sense. I can see how you might think that, but I wasn't spoiled, actually. I'd chalk it up to racial trauma. I'm sensitive to being misread.

ELENA: I don't understand.

GREG: My frustration. I mean it's not from entitlement. When I was in fifth or sixth grade, someone told me a racist joke that I never forgot. Want to hear it? It's pretty bad.

ELENA: Sure.

GREG: What do you call a Black astrophysicist?

ELENA: Yeah, I heard this one.

GREG: Right? But you don't have to have heard it. If you grew up in this country, you know the punchline without having to be told. At first, the punchline wasn't obvious to me. At that point, I was still naive enough to think there was more than one answer. I actually thought the joke was funny. Sad-funny, but funny because it was so absurd. I even went home and told my dad the joke. That's when he told me there was no escape. There's no amount of work I can do in this country to be accepted on my own terms. And it's funny because Americans are all about reinvention, right?

ELENA: Okay, but you have to admit things are better today than they were generations ago.

Fita enters holding an African mask over her face.

ELENA: Hello, young lady. How old are you? Do you want to take a walk with me, show me your room upstairs?

We hear the offstage cry of Cato's phone.

MS. CATO: [Offstage] Hello? Speaking. I believe we are still on schedule for the inspection. Right, I requested an escort. If you could have the officer meet us there, uh-huh, great. Thank you.

Charm for Enduring the Dark Night of the Soul

Franz Boll (1849–1879)
C. P. Robin (1821–1885)

First thank Charles-Philippe Robin for discovering
melanin, the supernatural source of your
blackness, your laughter, your ichor and irony.
Were it not for Western science, you might be just
an average person. Next, recognize Franz Boll,
the physiologist who discovered that the eyes'
cones and rods, once exposed, bleach bone-
white by a protein called rhodopsin, or "visual
purple," which enables us to see in differing
economies of light. Melanin and rhodopsin combine
in this charm to counter the veil of grouchiness
your melanin generates in the eyes of some
who have less of it to show. "Melanopsin" favors
blue-blacks and governs the body's rhythms on
and on until the break of dawn. This compound
coheres under pressure and smolders copper-bright
and sure as heat chewing the edges of records
from family plantations. For inside the history
of entitlement nuance is redacted and all is black
and white. One drop toward the margin, and
there's space for race understood as a theory
enacted. When melanin prompts little aggressions
in strangers, this charm will keep you from falling into
the collapsed star of their imagination and the haze
that grows around it like a cataract. This charm
employs melanopsin's magick power to move
entire tax bases to the suburbs. Its power to move
them back. Its power, too, to remove personal

liability in rejected college applications. This charm
will help you see patterns across time and industries.
       This is an anti-gaslighting charm.
Over-manifesting the power of melanopsin can cause
coffin bells to ring as you pass abandoned Negro
cemeteries, a condition commonly known as "too
black, too strong." After a spit take of Beaujolais
to purify your nightgown, let that purple rain cloud
the vision of evil eyes as you chant-rap the following:
*I know times are changing / It's time we all reach out
for something new / That means you, too.* This charm
will defend you from a metaphor for justice
that covers its eyes to truths that by its own
measure should be plain as daylight.

Beauty School Wig Head: The Marion Devotions

It could have been any number
of fever dream visitations—
this was around the time I became a girl
dad. I don't know what possessed me
to bring the Styrofoam wig head home.
It could have been Teresa Ávila, my
patron saint, her spectral presence,
implicit as any bias, that came to haunt
the beauty school wig head I
liberated from the museum of trash
bags that lined the curb on Fulton Mall.
Museum. As in altar to the muses
rising from objects appraised in
an alien tongue. At the time,
I would have called the wig head's
face sublime, fair, proportionally
ideal. In a word, Beautiful, in that sense
the majority culture calls *conventional.*
From the trash heap the wig head
caught my eye when a wailing fire
truck scuffed my optic nerve and flamed
the halo of a migraine. I was waiting
for the late bus home under a dunce
cap of light. Teresa Ávila, of course,
patron saint of headaches come to mock
the habit of mind I was inclined
to project onto the wig head. Namely,
that beauty is the residue we find
when color is stripped away. That
instead of color, I should praise
the thing that color leaves behind.

Security gates veiled the storefront.
Dead leaves and papier-mâchéd junk
mail clogged the doorway. That old
school of beauty was defunct, emptied
of its mirrors and lamps. What's left
was mere edifice with a for-rent
sign that read *Bring your imagination.*
The vacant storefront reminded me
of the graphic design studio
my mother owned in the late '70s.
She made her living as a commercial
artist, art she made to sell. She was a sub-
contractor for the Yellow Pages.
The bulk of her business, she made
display ads that were in turn sold
to plumbers, dentists, personal injury
lawyers. She called it piece-work, a term
I misspelled in my ear. A term
which kept her in protracted
labor day and night, contemplating
beauty at her tilted drafting desk.
Each quarter-column ad
was a stained-glass panel,
colors illuminating pages
to transfix consumers and proselytize
the merchants' creed. Her side
table held T-squares, X-Acto knives,
a cosmos of leads and markers.
Her fingers blackened like
a scribe's, she brought forth upon
blank pages of ginger,
taxicab, sunflower. The flare
at the center of my memory.

It's how the world looks
without the filter of my eyes.
Beauty as market share, as
coercive force. Beauty as capital,
its source and its demise.

*

Beauty is, I'm trying to say, not
the muse but the regime. The dreamer
is the subject of the dream.
Reputed to have been,
like my mother, a great beauty,
St. Teresa Ávila inspired in countless
men a frenzy to reproduce
her, the muse and mother of so many
inventions, so many versions of her
it hardly matters what she looked like,
only that the idea of her remains fruitful,
beauty as ticket to the carnival of witness
where one finds funhouse mirrors
in every stranger's eyes. Now that I
think of it, I never heard my father
call my mother beautiful,
though I have no doubt he found
the idea of her fruitful.

*

"You press the button," Kodak
claimed, "we'll do the rest."
The company's twentieth-
century dominion over film
processing and production meant
the childhoods of Boomers and Gen

X'ers the world over were
haunted by a woman named Shirley.
I found her photo in the darkroom
of my mother's studio and learned
without being told how Shirley's
spectral presence, implicit as any
bias, haunted birthdays, road trips,
barbecues and weddings,
by haunting the photos that would
define how these moments lived
in our memories. For years,
the "Shirley card"—named for
the first woman it featured—
governed the development of every
Kodacolor print. Technicians used
Shirley like a tuning fork
to "correct" colors in the photo-
finishing process, an innocent
stand-in for the skin
tones that would be offered
to the eye. Shirley, over the years,
was many women with one
thing in common. I learned
from her without being told, to see
in the key of her conventional beauty.

*

I'm afraid I looted this wig
head to work out my own
theories and memes, to work
out this dysmorphia the wig head
excites, and which beauty schools
still teach, that though I may be
comely, perhaps, by their rubrics

I could never be—nor find the history
that made me—beautiful unless I first
unlearn the beauty that is an
assimilation, subordination to a
lifeless ideal. For the beauty
of convention is lifeless even
to those who believe it
is attainable. If I could be
the forensic dreamer and breathe
her alive, this Styrofoam prop,
and give her the hue and tint
of life like Greek statues rescued
from the whitewash of time,
however ecstatic, my art
would nonetheless be
a mortician's paints. Some say
the pallor lubricates allure. Beauty
as fugitive, indescribable. Beauty
as a closed door.

                    *

There's a meme that pits
a closeup of Bernini's
Teresa against a tabloid
photo of Lindsay Lohan
blissed-out in her passenger
seat after kicking it
at da club. Her hoody,
the posture of repose,
the inglorious source of her
slack jaw, all erode
the innocence I was taught
that kind of beauty must
convey. The symmetry

between Bernini's *Teresa*
and Blissed-Lindsay
is uncanny, as if it occurs
by accident and not by
templated design—the same
woman multiplied, producing
a public of one mind. Lohan's
repute as a troubled
starlet and the schadenfreude
that is her fortune cast both
as mute martyrs to beauty,
both arrested in an attempt
to take flight. Lohan bleached
to the bone in the blitz
of the paparazzi's light. Teresa
in the tradition of women whom
men have imagined passive or
whom men have turned to stone.

*

Who wouldn't want to be
a white woman in ecstasy?
Is ecstasy representable in any
other form? *I'll have what she's having*,
the lady at the neighboring table
in the diner says in that famous
film by Nora Ephron.
In a quiet moment of reflection
once, my father mused, "How do
ugly people make love?"
What I took from that, more than
the distastefulness of the comment,
was a glimpse of my father's
empowered self-image. I don't think

I've ever called myself beautiful
except in defiance.

*

When Jane Fonda plays Saint
Teresa as Barbarella,
her confessor, male, early
fifties, tucks her in beneath
the rubber sheet of his
excessive pleasure machine,
intending to torture her
heteronormatively, flood her
nervous system with dopamine
until she's mad, but she
absorbs it. Her tolerance for
ecstasy exceeds his capacity
to deliver it. What will she do
now that man is insufficient
to the task? Eventually,
my mother left my father,
a move incomprehensible
to me because it made her
happiness independent
of our observation.

*

As birthday gifts go, my father
unwrapping a studio photograph
of her nude displayed
a logic that escaped me then and
escapes me now. It was the '70s,
is all I can say. Meeting sight-
lines from the open door of

my parents' boudoir,
the gallery-sized picture
facing my dad's side of the bed—
the driver's side if it were a car—
announced his Duchess
to a generation of houseguests
perusing the living
museum of our three-bedroom
ranch home. In the photo,
my mom faces forward
with her left shoulder canted
gently toward the camera. (It's not
the same posture exactly, but
Prince's self-titled album
cover evokes tangled associations
and gives me conflicting shivers.)
Her right hand's armadilloed
in a silver gauntlet. A sword
gripped, tip-down in a posture
of surrender so that the cross guard
underscores her collarbone, a Jesus
piece that could make her an actual
martyr. The blade, surgical, is a flash
of light from a cracked door. Whether
it is being drawn or sheathed,
it hums with inertia like a train rail.
But what I noticed as a kid was
the way her chin curtseyed to meet
her left shoulder as if refusing
someone's touch or, given her
lowered lids, transforming
surrender into ecstasy—a word
I could have only used in irony
like the scraps of costume armor,
the courtly incongruity of it, given

to her in a pretense of protection
from what.

*

This was not my mother,
unless the staging was her idea, an
allusion to Caravaggio's *Saint
Catherine of Alexandria*, the martyr
kneeling beside the wheel
that failed to break her,
holding the sword
that would take off with
her head. Or could it be a more
subtle reference to *Judith
Slaying Holofernes* by
Gentileschi, the artist who,
instead of relenting,
instead of giving up
her insistence that her
testimony was true,
endured thumbscrews that
were meant to break her
resolve, break her refusal to recant,
her refusal to exonerate her
rapist in court, as instead, she
chanted through the pain,
È vero, è vero, è vero?
(It's true, it's true, it's true.)
My mother could have been jamming
this beauty signal by ironizing
the violence of an art history
in which, as an artist, at any rate,
she could not exist.
What if, thinking of Gentileschi,

I imagined my mom drawing
her sword from the stone
of vengeance? Would the mash-up
make for a gothic soul aesthetic,
rip a rabbit hole in the Western
rules of seeing wide enough
to hold a wonderland of color?
My mother became an artist,
I believe, because she wanted
to wield beauty as a transitive verb.
Gifted, she became her gift because
my father Midas found her
becoming. He called her redbone.
High yellow. The color of parchment,
the legal pad I scratch on like
a gilt manuscript. The nicotine
on his fingertips staining
everything he and I hold dear.

*

I learned without being told
to love the fictions women
portrayed in the movies
my father loved. Tamara
Dobson as Cleopatra
Jones, who gives a boy
like me a dollar
to protect her muscle
car purring at the corner.
Vonetta McGee hauling bags
of cash, on the lam.
Yet, neither Vonetta,
Tamara, Teresa,
Lindsay nor even

the idea of the real
Egyptian queen Jones
bears in her fictional
name bears evidence
of flex or perspiration
the way Bernini's *Teresa*
is veiled in a humorless
mystique, a fake-ID face
ageless as the obsidian
that cracketh not. I want to
imagine the wig head alive,
like an African mask. I want
to imagine my mother's inner life,
not because she's a woman,
but because the fiction
of her I have inherited
cannot imagine me. Gender
as occlusion. My mother is a mirror
in which I cannot appear.

*

My mother's
beauty replaced her
face. I almost said
"my" face—mercy—
as if I could know
life through her eyes.
It troubles
me that I'll never know
what she was
like before she made me
me. A stranger like the bus
driver I only knew through
the mail slot of her rearview

mirror, whose alto guided
my routine home.
Why did I keep it,
the wig head I held in my lap
like an infant? Not
as maidenhead or patron
saint. More than
gorgon or ornament
or effigy, but to summon
my love for what, I suppose,
by beauty I must mean
all that is woman in me.

Magnificat

Monterchi, a village named for a mountain named for Hercules,
before names was known for contagious fertility, and twice since

church fathers blamed human weakness, want and conflict
on Eve's sin, and ordained Diana's altars and her magnificence

destroyed and overwritten, the earth inside the mountain kicked.
Nothing happens once. Even the infinite is a rhythm, a pulse,

the image of itself in all things repeated. Contractions, the landscape
in sympathetic labor with *Madonna del Parto*, a painting, the way a fossil

is a rock. Her baby bump echoes the hill of Tepeyac where Juan Diego
reimagined Tonantzin as La Morenita, Our Lady of Guadalupe;

her affect flat as Mt. Carmel where hermits heard wind crying Mary—
the music in Piero's painting in Monterchi pushes the envelope

of public art. Said to protect expecting pilgrims, this quattrocento
fresco's ultrasound revealed beneath the pregnant virgin another layer

bearing Mary by an earlier master, babe already at the breast.
Like cities upon cities, form reflects Mary's depth, and this palimpsest

buries and nurtures its stories at once. When Nature's seismic choir
magnified the earth, broke it like water, glassy and fragile, the sylvan

chapel's load-bearing saint was at last emancipated and kissed
between wind-drunk cypresses by an ardent sun. She from ruin,

carried like a shelter, protected by whom she protects: the pious
who claimed daylight quickened beneath pigment the adrenaline

in Piero's latent cartoons. The artist tutored by Euclid, Pythagoras,
Al-Khwarizmi, might have pictured this bride of a double groom

spooked by the angel at the palm tree. "Would that I died before this,"
Mary laments in the Quran, which shows her, nevertheless, persist

in counting down to anno domini. Fun fact, the word for "womb"
in Hebrew also means compassion. Imagine, before using the Baptist

baby John to gender-reveal Jesus, Mary asking Elizabeth's
thoughts on Hecuba, say, getting her girls to lay in wait and scoop

the eyes of the king who heaved her son from a parapet (not often
was Mary without a book) or sharing fears of becoming a coffin.

Or sharing our mothers' fear of the beloved child slain by a cop
who claims his fear is proof of his heroism. Piero enshrined

her, a proto-feminist ode to labor, sovereign as thrice-wed Erzulie
who commands men to venerate the source of creation.

Working seven days, Piero hoped to have God the Goddess's kind
of compassion. He wanted to make a thing so well it grows holy,

becomes the beholder, and the Creator becomes the thing beheld.
The mural announced her pronouns when she outlived the latest quake.

As if to be recognized as a woman she had to endure trauma.
In sundry tongues below her, prayers in baskets since have spelled

requests like quizzes she might check for penmanship and grammar.
Inside her sunless classroom now, every pupil swells to grasp the lectures

she radiates. The schoolhouse-turned-gallery is a compromise, a halfway
home where she may convalesce in calming UV lights while the search

for her forever home continues. One brainchild town fathers
had was to lease her like a sideshow Venus to underwrite a new church.

A wall of mothers rose in her defense. And when those same powers
that be invited artists in Florence to restore her, locals say the mothers

laid their bodies in the street. Not to weep or pray the hog's
hair brushwork remain chaste nor that the angels' true colors

not streak a sad mascara from their pinions to the pleats of their frocks.
Not in repent but as an athlete genuflects, the *Madonna*'s host

of votaries who, like madres de los desaparecidos, would spare no cost
defending the glory Vestals bricked inside cathedral walls lost

their lives achieving, to show where beat the *Madonna*'s infinite heart.
Inside the matrix of their care, she'd be more than just a work of art.

Theater Selfie

At Richard Rodgers Theatre, I shrank my face to the box
office window and confessed to the Lucite's voice-vent
that I'd told my wife a lie. I had hidden no Christmas gifts
in the basement nor yet acquired tickets to *Hamilton*
for my youngest as I'd boasted I would. Oblivious to cost,
I was a hostage to the season and my ego, forced to drain
the ATM for my deliverance. The ticket guy pshawed and,
like a chilly neighbor, acknowledged me enough to punctuate
his snub. But the seat map online, I pleaded, showed several
vacant dots in March. No seats, he snapped, and we went on
like this until I looked it up on my phone. Those? He snarled,
you can't—his pause—its meaning irretrievable now—
was heavy with the ghosts of Broadway's sins. It was as if a voice
offstage was force-feeding him the line: *You can't afford those.*
His cheeks ripened to prove he'd heard it just
as I'd heard it, but that, this time maybe, he'd heard it *in the way*
that I'd heard it. Face frozen, his eyes went floodlight,
making me suddenly real. The veil had fallen between us,
and we two stood outside the magic. We were our only audience.
As one trained in this hackneyed improv, I knew that I might
dress the specter of his fear in comedy to save him. I needed
to draw him out of his head. You got kids? I asked.
He nodded, but I needed to hear the emotion in his voice.
What are you gunna do, huh? I laughed. It's like, what do you want
from me? Am I right? And he mirrored me, shaking his head:
The things we do. He asked if I could bring my kid next Tuesday.
Hells yeah, I said, careful to stay in character, though
I wasn't sure where he was taking us. He bent to root
beneath his desk. Then the Lucite spit two miracles

he must have set aside for someone else. The selfie
we took that day tells a partial story. You see us, all teeth
and safe as bros. You see me holding the tickets like a peace sign,
but you could never guess the price we paid to get them.

Dramaturgy for the Bullet

Lights up, the slow wipe of darkness by an empty swing listing in fog.

The following voice-overs are in the public domain and can be used in both romantic and tragic adaptations:

911 CALLER: It's probably fake, but you know what, it's scaring the shit out of me.
911 CALLER: He's sitting on a swing right now.
DISPATCH: There's a Black male sitting on a swing.

The child actor pretends not to hear the sirens.

The child actor pretends not to recognize the monologic of the bullet's one-liner.

Music is diegetic. Narration is diegetic. Everything everywhere is diegetic.

The child actor pretends to play a game. Born for this role, he makes it look real. It is real. Overcast. Light contrasts on the set: sidewalk, grass, gazebo. The audience, remote, watches through a camera hunched like a gargoyle and bolted to the rec center's façade across the street. The child actor pretends to be a cowboy, reading lines that were not intended for him. The prop, a supporting character, forgets its lines. *Bang-bang*, the child actor whispers.

This is a live performance.

There are no bad props. Only bad actors. When the fourth wall is blue, bad actors are protected from critical review. When the fourth wall is a flag, bad actors are protected by the Second Amendment.

The Justice Department says the child actor's prop is "visually virtually indistinguishable" from a real gun.

Bad actors drive their cruiser onto the grass and leap out to prove who has the faster draw. In two seconds flat the child actor gives the performance of a lifetime. Justice is not the critical rubric for this tragedy. The video will not do it justice. Justice will not be done.

For contrast, refer to the October 21, 2021, adaptation staged at Bonanza Creek Ranch in Bonanza City, New Mexico, featuring the bullet in a tragicomic performance.

Fade in: dusty saloon doors weep rusty in the wind.

Set the cinematographer behind her camera to line up her shot. The bad actor aims his prop gun at her and pretends to shoot. His face is pained with laughter. The bullet appears, confused, to everyone's surpise, in the wrong scene, on the wrong set.

The bad actor shoots the cinematographer before she shoots him. This is a Western. The fastest actor wins. This is an actor-involved shooting.

The weight of a watch battery, the bullet has no wardrobe requirements. It brings its own metal jacket.

Supplement:
The seminal American performance took place at the opera house in Livermore, Kentucky, 1911. Staging the show for themselves, the audience kindled the footlights for effect and tied the lifeless body of their lead actor to the existing set onstage. The lead role of Will Potter, a Black man accused of attempting to murder a white man who had instigated a poolroom brawl, was played by himself. The lead role is a prop. The audience propped up Will Potter like a marionette without strings, and, from the orchestra pit, let their instruments resound. Bullets took to the air like notes lifted from sheet music, making a percussive accompaniment to Will Potter's finale. The music was diegetic, though it could have been mistaken for thunderous applause. The audience threw roses. The roses, too, were bullets.

[Erasure]

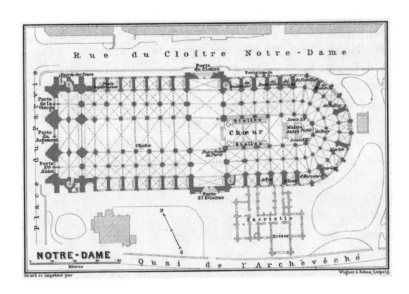

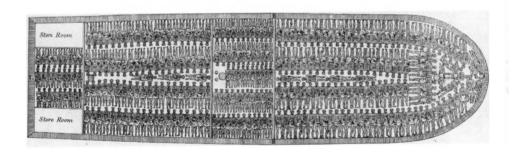

Dragonflies

When my nephew pudges with his saggy pumpkin
face, and I think maybe it's his mouth he's got
around some gewgaw from the floor, I want
to pry his trap open, but he won't budge. It's
like his lips are sewn shut in some horror-flick
affliction, which is so freaking cute I wish I could
Cookie Monster his whole head. He gets it
from our side, his mouth almighty, for we Pardlo men
have been known to show less sense than appetite.
Pop claimed I used to hum in protest the final bars
of the Marseillaise or at least that's what he
heard when, attacked by "dragonflies," as he
called it, as in *that boy got the dragonflies*—
the kind fictive as the boogeyman, needles stitching
shut the pieholes of chatterboxes and tattletales,
having mesmerized the brats like flying spoons
of tapioca—I used to zip it as if I had Houdini
in there or like my tongue was busy putting boat
knots in phantom maraschino stems. *Boy looks like
a monkey on a cupcake!* the old man would say, none
of which rings a bell, but he swore it's true, my face.
I must have worn that foolish grin to death as
every hunger in our house was second to his,
my old man fearing, perhaps like Goya's *Saturn*,
his dominion's decline, and though he'd taunt me,
refused to let him see me cry.

She Shed

If he wishes to find out whether she is endowed with a witch's power of preserving silence, let him take note whether she is able to shed tears when standing in his presence, or when being tortured . . . if she be a witch she will not be able to weep: although she will assume a tearful aspect and smear her cheeks and eyes with spittle to make it appear that she is weeping; wherefore she must be closely watched by the attendants.

—*Hammer of the Witches* (1489)

Yet some have been known to make a tearless weeping their métier, thus giving birth to the blues. Others weep like ceramic Madonnas, in viscous ruby beads. A nesting impulse, some are rumored to retreat to a place of contemplation, a spiritual cloister and therein cry out in tongues. Yet my mother only wept in anger. Her mother only wept in blood. Yet it has never been proven she could place two tears in a bucket. Cameras could not corroborate her in distress, though inmates in neighboring cells heard Sandra Bland drowning in midair. At Gorée, a room the size of a walk-in closet was meant to hold dozens new to bleeding until impregnated by visiting merchants to whom they were offered as party favors. Yet not a single painting depicts them in recoil. Among them there is misery enough, yet nowhere is it recorded that any of them wept.

Law & Order

[If] by intentional threats or menace of some violence such as
looking at a person in a leering manner, that is, in some sort
of sly or threatening or suggestive manner; watching one and
then following one, he causes another to reasonably apprehend
imminent danger, and by such conduct causes one to become
frightened and run or causes one to do otherwise than he would
have done, then he is guilty of an assault.

—NORTH CAROLINA SUPERIOR COURT
JUDGE FRANK M. ARMSTRONG'S INSTRUCTIONS
TO THE JURY, 1952

From the court's and seventeen-year-old Miss Willa Jean Boswell's
perspectives, everything will have happened as she
describes it, and as the prosecutor will have advised her to
describe it for the Yanceyville jury when this third of four
trials adjourns. She is telling it like she told her
father and brothers: Matt Ingram's jalopy appeared
on the plantation road she took to join them—Daddy
and them—in the field. They was picking tobacco,
she's saying, one of the many facts that will be true in each
trial as it was that day in June of '51. True as her dungarees
and plaid shirt, the broad hat under which, her hair. The long-
handled hoe shouldered like a rifle for the fields where she,
that particular morning, was bound. Ingram hung his whole head
out the window as he drove by, she is about to say.
Real slow-like, barely any dustup. He never done like that
before. She may be remembering how Ingram vanished
when he drove on around the bend, when she heard his engine go
dead, and she ran for the safety of her kin. She didn't see him
leave the car, she can't say, but there he was, in the field,

76

so close, maybe—the prosecutor will have helped her reckon—
seventy feet or so. Like, say, from the doors of the church
to the pulpit. Ingram stopped at some plum bushes, watched her
in silence, the judge prompts. She knows Matt—"Mack," everybody
calls him—as a good Negro, a reputation that requires a talent
for being present and absent at once, the only way a man like him
could imagine a fate beyond sharecropping, by scrubbing traces
of plot and motive from his life story to show he had no designs
on the history that belongs to the men whose order the law maintains.
That's why his *leer*—her testimony in the fourth trial will record it
as a *leer*—was so menacing, she will have meant to say, shaken, weeping,
still scared. As everyone knows, Ingram will be charged with assault
with intent to rape. Less certain is that, on appeal, two years from now,
he'll be sentenced to time served. His innocence will have been proven
irrelevant. His family—wife, nine children—bankrupted,
dispossessed, dispersed. The mortgage on his farm, foreclosed.
At this point in Willa Jean's testimony, as Ingram listens, he knows
he is still searching for Mr. Boswell, hoping to borrow a trailer,
as he has often done, and that this time will be the last because
he knows he will leave his car and find some shade by the plum
bushes where he can scan the field to see where Boswell and his boys
might be working—he can even see himself in Willa Jean's
story still wondering, though now he knows, who is that strange boy
with the big hat and the hoe, and where is he off to in such a hurry.

Spectral Evidence

The black man's Voice was hough and goustie.

—*Saducismus Triumphatus* (1681)

Declares that on Harvest last, the Devil in the shape of a Black man

 had the most aggressive face that his eyes were bugging out

After the declarant had gone to bed, the Black man
 visited his neighborhood in the shape of a Black man running

  away that the Black man looks like a bad dude

 who might be on something

Declares that the Black man's name is Ejoall that the Black man's
 Clothes were Black
  his feet were cloven
    he looked like a demon before him

  that the Black man

did put pins in the Picture of Wax In the shape of a Black man the
 Black man

came in and called the declarant quietly by his name

  staring right through him
  and tossed him around like Hulk Hogan with a ragdoll

Declares that the Devil in the shape of a Black man lay with her in the Bed under the Clothes   that the Black man

                    was a woman disappearing in and out of view

Declares that the Black man was a fourteen-year-old boy who

came to her Mother's House and required the Declarant
to give herself up to him

        that she did give herself to the Black man

that the Black man whistled and   that the Black man was
        threatening

to escape

[Erasure]

REPORT 6 OF THE COUNCIL ON SCIENCE AND PUBLIC HEALTH (A-09) Use of Tasers® by Law Enforcement Agencies (Reference Committee D)

Although not a validated diagnostic entity in either the International Classification of Diseases or the *Diagnostic and Statistical Manual of Mental Disorders*, "excited delirium" is a widely accepted entity in forensic pathology and is cited by medical examiners to explain the sudden in-custody deaths of individuals who are combative and in a highly agitated state. Excited delirium is broadly defined as a state of agitation, excitability, paranoia, aggression, and apparent immunity to pain, often associated with stimulant use and certain psychiatric disorders. The signs and symptoms typically ascribed to "excited delirium" include bizarre or violent behavior, hyperactivity, hyperthermia, confusion, great strength, sweating and removal of clothing, and imperviousness to pain. Speculation about triggering factors include [*sic*] sudden and intense activation of the sympathetic nervous system, with hyperthermia, and/or acidosis, which could trigger life-threatening arrhythmias in susceptible individuals. Biochemical studies have shown alterations in the function of dopamine neurons and specific gene activation products in the central nervous system of such individuals. The intense pain associated with Taser® exposure, the psychological distress of incapacitation, and hazards associated with various restraint methods also could contribute.

(2009)

Metaphor

To transfer or carry, as a man might carry
his namesake in his arms or on shoulders cheering, "we
bad, uh-huh, we bad!" as my father did when he saw himself
in me. As I came of age, however, I thought my father was,
in the sense that means *to hamper or impede*,
an embarrassment, which is, as all language is
essentially, a metaphor. I. A. Richards says a metaphor
consists of a tenor and a vehicle. My father would
point out that he's using a metaphor
to define metaphors, a literalization, like the relic
to the corpse. Like when Richards asks himself
if a wooden leg is a metaphor
for a wooden leg. My dad, Gregory Pardlo, Sr.,
before he died, lost his leg to diabetes. Even though he
himself would be the only person to see it, he insisted
that the prosthesis precisely match
his skin tone. The same guy who gave me
a Hot Wheels car for Christmas. A joke, see. He'd promised
me a car when I turned sixteen. It shimmers on my
desk now, a kitschy muse with shark's teeth decals behind
the wheel wells. Before he died, I told him I would have
preferred a Matchbox car packaged in an actual matchbox,
literalizing the figurative commingling of tenor and vehicle,
more metonym than metaphor, a pedigree, in other words.
He told me to get the stick out of my ass. Greg Pardlo
is dead. Long live Greg Pardlo.

Convertible

My pop let me steer when I was small
enough to snug between his belly and the wheel.
Any random intersection, he might hoist
me across the hand brake onto his lap to pilot
the wagon before returning me to earth.
                    As I got older, he'd make me
steer while he lit a smoke or shed his jacket.

His ashes arrived in a cardboard carton with
shipping labels and barcode, heavy enough
to trigger the seat belt alarm as we clipped home,
honeysuckle in the air, from the post office.
A reasonable person would have put the box
on the floor, but I—you know already, don't you?
I held him in my lap. "You're mine," I told
the box of dad dust, lifting my hands occasionally,
reckless to the wind, tempting the evening, swinging
our private chariot of steel and bone.

Multiple Choices for Ell Persons

Ell Persons, a Negro woodcutter, lived in a cabin in the woods off Macon Road. He often saw the blonde girl riding her bicycle to school in the morning because he walked the same route each day to the mill.

From sentences 1 and 2, you might predict this story will end tragically because:

A) The subject has an unusual name.
B) We are taught that Black men either overachieve or die tragically.
C) The term "Negro woodcutter" is used unironically.
D) It involves an interaction between a Black man and a white girl.

Driving down Beale Street in their pickup, lynchers threw Ell Persons's burned and earless head at a group of Black people and shouted:

A) How do you like your brown-eyed boy?
B) Take this with our compliments!
C) Here's proof Orpheus sings the blues!
D) There are good people on both sides!

Ten thousand people attended the picnic because:

A) The time and location had been announced in the Memphis papers.
B) Picnickers wanted relics of the saint.
C) They wanted to remind each other, "This is not who we are."
D) They wanted to see justice served.

When Antoinette Rappel's body was found in the woods off the county road, beheaded and sexually assaulted, investigators believed the assailant was white because:

A) There was no indication of struggle at the crime scene.
B) Articles of men's clothing left at the scene suggested the assailant was a man of means.
C) There was nothing to implicate any of the Black residents in the area.
D) All of the above.

One day at work, Persons told his boss's wife that she had appeared in a dream of his. Mrs. Brooks then told her husband, E. J. Brooks, who recalled this disturbing detail when he learned that Persons had been questioned in the Rappel case. When Brooks informed Sheriff Mike Tate that Persons had once frightened Mrs. Brooks in this way, although Persons had already been questioned and ruled out twice before, Sheriff Tate said the evidence "showed that Persons was a [N]egro capable of committing a crime such as the Rappel murder. It gave us the first inkling of his brutish proclivities, and we lost no time taking him into custody."

In addition to his confession, evidence used to indict Ell Persons included:

A) A tip by a deaf-mute whom the white men in town knew only as "Dummy."
B) An optographic image of Persons found in Antoinette Rappel's eye.
C) The pressure on Sheriff Mike Tate to solve the murder.
D) All of the above.

Ell Persons confessed because:

A) Sheriff Mike Tate couldn't be wrong a third time.
B) Sheriff Mike Tate and Detectives Brunner and Hoyle tortured him.
C) He felt pity for the Rappel girl.
D) He knew the story of Tituba.

Giornata (the work): The Essay on Fidelity

Bud-sized flames popsicle the wicks of a wax two
and one atop a Dominican cake. With tango arms
we hold the wedding knife, renew the annual gibes.
Is it devotion or inertia keeps us together? Why split
gray hairs? Our marriage is old enough to drink.
Instead of babies we make banana bread and feed
our instruments of joy. We play a game we call "That's
Yo Child!" and chase the minotaur until we're breathless.
Some loves were born connected by an infinite thread.
Our thread is kinked with fisherman's knots and a rusty
hook chumming along my 175 pounds of fear, for isn't
love a kind of fear, the inner infant that's just a tar baby
for heartbreak? And as our mingled breath exhausts
the candles, an island of Whitneys rises in song, and drags
back all my forgotten loves, fish wrapped across
whitecaps and sea spray salting the shores craggy as the stiff
peaks of meringue that frame the faces—yours, mine—
the bakery has airbrushed across this moist and delectable
confection we now jab at each other's kissers fork by fork.

2.

Bathing in the milk light of the boob tube in a house
that moved like a shipwreck with curtains that sieved
wind through midnight portals, I wormed my finger down
the back of my jammies to see what the fuss was about.
For once my dad's asthma had not announced him
like Darth Vader emerging from the corridor's murk.
His scalpel-eyes flayed me clean as an X-ray, a cartoon
cat struck by lightning. In that moment, gravity wanted
nothing to do with me, which let me suspect myself
an angel, holy, holy, as I considered the tenders of my
dust-to-dust until disgust sandbagged my thought balloon
and I tsked that boy on the floor watching TV with his
finger in his ass. My macho cowardice would not let me
recognize that boy as me and said no man, for health
or pleasure (twin measures of the body's weakness),
should plunder the pervious mercy of his dark side.
I wore that taboo like a cone collar. The other day,
from an anesthetized twilight on a gurney,
I once again lay on my side weightless with eyes glued
to a TV screen, and let a greased lens gerbil its way
through my colon, and thought of you, Dear Lord
Vader, family history my doctor fears. As I introspect
with borrowed vision, now I weep for you and pray
for you and for me, and for boys like us taught
to be indifferent to the spirit within.

4.

An old husband's tale reckons that witches are children
of sexless angels and their human eunuchs, angels
whose self-restraint was inversely proportional to the power
to silence their victims. Papa's maybes of a Zeus-like
ravishment from above. Immaculate. Paul said women
should wear an "authority" on their heads, by which he meant a veil,
like a force field to protect them from lustful angels. Adam
copped angel lust from those selfsame freaky mayflies
who by turns learned their grift at God's extensive
digit bulbing like molten glass at the end of a blowpipe.
God got his from Greeks. Thus completes, like a network
of shell companies, the history of qualified
immunity. Every man should learn to balance a set of books
that looks like an anvil—instead of a veil—on our heads
for posture in the figurative sense, standing in God's eyes
where God, like the future, is female—a prophylactic
against patriarchy, a cork stopper in the mouth of a gun.

6.

My father Bacchus wanted a daughter instead of me.
He felt the threat a son implies, and took you, my infant
virility, scarf-skin like a halo, angel of my innocence
fore-fledged. Before the ritual, there was guilt. You were
vestigial as the divot beneath my nose where the angel pinched
my lips in binding silence. Would I see myself in style or fit
if I encountered you, my soul, draped like a lost mitten
on a fencepost? Tattered as a moth-eaten turtleneck.
       Hood like the hood of a headsman.
If you were re-appended, would you lisp like chiffon
or crunch like corduroy? You are the macho my father's
dream foretold—he who, in the end, was like a son to me,
whose own member circumscribed a foreshortened life
story mine was intended to resemble. My forebear, the brutal
gardener. He who conjured the corona must have foreseen
his own eclipse, and standing on ceremony, found at hand
a means to get my sex to bleed.

7.

Shovel of Brooks's "The Lovers of the Poor"

Only with a preacher who says *up in here* instead of *herein*.
Our vows could reference calla lilies and the snowy pistils they
jab ardently at our faces. Their linty, foul-mouthed kiss
could litter satin tablecloths white as bee-boxes and
we'd crowd-buzz self-invented as love bugs built to coddle,
not sting. Otherwise, we'll karaoke euphemisms for *civil* and
ceremony, refrain from moderation, charge our senses with assault.

9.

The swear jar isn't empty. Full of flowers
instead of coins it curses a bouquet
of love-me-nots, a tangled vine of credit
extended to one most likely to default.
Such a trifling bargain, flowers for mercy.
O Nature, predatory lender!
Risk is the commuter bus I ride between damnation
and wonder, arrival and departure marking
the same location. *Give me chastity,*
O Lord, as the Berber Saint says, but stitch my wounds
loosely for miracle and sin are kindred.
Both are hatched from broken law.

10

The famous Negro athlete doubts the planet
is round and ripe. Its magnetic navel
adrift escapes like leaves turned dryly
underfoot. The moon, so
immense you can smell its breath,
demands its sugar like your Great-
Aunt Ginny. A flame deflates atop
a skull. Swisher-sweet, this scent, so many
flies. Éluard writes, "the Earth
is blue like an orange." Watch it tremolo,
as on a Globetrotter's finger, in the smoke-
filled soap bubble that dances iridescent
in space. She aims the emberred butt
of her cigarette at the moon in a puddle.
Its extinction makes the sound of nothing but net.

Acknowledgments

"Theater Selfie" (p. 68), initially published as "At Richard Rodgers
    Theatre," *The Yale Review*
"Occult," *Paris Review*
"Allegory," *The New Yorker*
"Giornata 6," Poem-A-Day (Arthur Sze, ed.)
"Giornata 9," appeared as "Giornata 11," Poem-A-Day (Monica Youn, ed.)
"Giornata 10," *The New Republic*
"Epistemology of the Phone Booth," Poem-A-Day (Alex Dmitrov, ed.)
"Metaphor" and "Convertible," *The Fight & The Fiddle*
"The Essay on Faith," *American Poetry Review*
"In the Name of the Mother," appears as "A Surname to Honor Their
    Mother" in *The 1619 Project: A New Origin Story*

I gratefully acknowledge the following collaborators, chief among them
Marion Wrenn, my partner in thought, without whom many of these poems
would not exist. Vievee Francis, whose work and friendship have been the
source of my education for the better part of a decade. Airea Dee Matthews,
who defines for me what it means to think courageously and independently.
Friends and readers whose care urged this project forward at crucial moments:
Kristin Mathis, Joanna Settle, Elisa Albert, Susan Briante, Baba Badji, Colin
Channer, Chad Rutkowski and Jackie Neale. I'd also like to thank my col-
leagues and students at Rutgers University–Camden, my colleagues and stu-
dents at NYU Abu Dhabi, the Fine Arts Work Center and PEN America. I am
grateful for material support from the Guggenheim Foundation, the Civitella
Ranieri Foundation, the Cullman Center of the New York Public Library and
the New York Institute for the Humanities. Foremost, I thank my family:
Ginger, Sara, Fita and Oliver. This has always been a team effort.

Bibliography

Baer, Ulrich. *Spectral Evidence: The Photography of Trauma.* Cambridge, Mass.: MIT Press, 2002.

Berry, Mary Frances. "'Reckless Eyeballing': The Matt Ingram Case and the Denial of African American Sexual Freedom." *The Journal of African American History* 93, no. 2 (2008): 223–34.

Bodin, Jean. *On the Demon-Mania of Witches.* 1580. Trans. Randy A. Scott. Toronto: Centre for Renaissance and Reformation Studies, 1995.

Bressler, Raymond George, and Richard A. King. *Markets, Prices, and Interregional Trade.* Belize: Norman-Weathers Printing Co., 1970.

(burninglyekisses). "Murder of 15 Year Old Leads to Lynching (Unresolved)—1917." Reddit, 2020. https://www.reddit.com/r/UnresolvedMysteries/comments/kupn41/murder_of_15_year_old_leads_to_lynching/.

Cixous, Hélène. "The Laugh of the Medusa." Trans. Keith Cohen and Paula Cohen. *Signs* 1, no. 4 (1976): 875–93.

Cureau de la Chambre, Marin. *The Characters of the Passions.* London: Tho. Newcomb, 1650.

Dorsky, Nathaniel. *Devotional Cinema.* Willits and Berkeley, Calif.: Tuumba Press, 2003.

Durkheim, Émile. *The Elementary Forms of the Religious Life.* Oxford: Oxford University Press, 1912.

Fields, Karen E., and Barbara J. Fields. *Racecraft: The Soul of Inequality in American Life.* New York: Verso, 2022.

Gonzales Rose, Jasmine B. "Racial Character Evidence in Police Killing Cases." *Wisconsin Law Review* 369 (2018). https://scholarship.law.bu.edu/faculty_scholarship/997.

Haley, Sarah. *No Mercy Here: Gender, Punishment, and the Making of Jim Crow Modernity.* Chapel Hill: University of North Carolina Press, 2019.

Hall, Kim F. *Things of Darkness: Economies of Race and Gender in Early Modern England*. Ithaca, N.Y.: Cornell University Press, 1995.

hooks, bell. *Art on My Mind: Visual Politics*. New York: New Press, 1995.

Hurston, Zora Neale. *Tell My Horse: Voodoo and Life in Haiti and Jamaica*. 1938. Berkeley, Calif.: Turtle Island, 1981.

Jay, Martin. "Scopic Regimes of Modernity." In *Vision and Visuality*, ed. Hal Foster, pp. 3–23. Seattle: Bay Press, 1988.

Kramer, Heinrich, and Jacob Sprenger. *Malleus Maleficarum: The Witch Hammer*. 1487. Trans. Montague Summers. 1928; Martino Fine Books, 2011.

Lewis, C. S. *Screwtape Letters*. 1942. New York: HarperOne, 2015.

Lindsay, Vachel. *The Congo and Other Poems*. New York: Macmillan, 1914.

Mirzoeff, Nicholas. *An Introduction to Visual Culture*. Oxford: Routledge, 1999.

Mitchell, Koritha. *Living with Lyching: African American Lynching Plays, Performance, and Citizenship, 1890–1930*. Champaign: University of Illinois Press, 2012.

Needham, Rodney. *Primordial Characters*. Charlottesville: University Press of Virginia, 1978.

Rauch, Angelika. "The *Trauerspiel* of the Prostituted Body, or Woman as Allegory of Modernity," *Cultural Critique* 10 (Autumn 1988): 77–88.

Rosenthal, Bernard. *Records of the Salem Witch-Hunt*. Cambridge: Cambridge University Press, 2009.

Schiff, Stacy. *The Witches: Salem, 1692*. New York: Back Bay Books, 2015.

Sharpe, Christina. *In the Wake: On Blackness and Being*. Durham, N.C.: Duke University Press, 2016.

Taylor, Leila. *Darkly: Black History and America's Gothic Soul*. London: Repeater Books, 2019.

Tillet, Salamishah. *Sites of Slavery: Citizenship and Racial Democracy in the Post–Civil Rights Imagination*. Durham, N.C.: Duke University Press, 2012.

Vandiver, Margaret. *Lethal Punishment: Lynchings and Legal Executions in the South*. New Brunswick, N.J.: Rutgers University Press, 2005.

Warner, Marina. *Alone of All Her Sex: The Myth and the Cult of the Virgin Mary*. New York: Alfred A. Knopf, 1976.

Wilkerson, Isabel. *Caste: The Origins of Our Discontents*. New York: Random House, 2020.

Williams, Joseph J. *Psychic Phenomena of Jamaica*. New York: Dial Press, 1935.

Winston, George T. "The Relation of the Whites to the Negroes." *The Annals of the American Academy of Political and Social Science* 18 (1901): 105–18.

Wright, Michelle M. *Physics of Blackness: Beyond the Middle Passage Epistemology*. Minneapolis: University of Minnesota Press, 2015.

Young, Darius. "'The Saving of Black America's Body and White America's Soul': The Lynching of Ell Persons and the Rise of Black Activism in Memphis." In *An Unseen Light: Black Struggles for Freedom in Memphis, Tennessee*, ed. Aram Goudsouzian and Charles W. McKinney, Jr., pp. 39–60. Lexington: University Press of Kentucky, 2018.

Page 22: Table from Kelly M. Hoffman, Sophie Trawalter, Jordan R. Axt and M. Norman Oliver, "Racial Bias in Pain Assessment and Treatment Recommendations, and False Beliefs About Biological Differences Between Blacks and Whites," *Proceedings of the National Academy of Sciences* 113, no. 16 (2016): 4296–4301.

Page 33: Page from George T. Winston, "The Relation of the Whites to the Negroes," *The Annals of the American Academy of Political and Social Science* 18 (1901): 112.

Page 73: (*top*) Courtesy of Antiqua Print Gallery / Alamy Stock Photo; (*bottom*) Drawing by the Plymouth Chapter of the Society for Effecting the Abolition of the Slave Trade, 1788, Wikimedia Commons.

Gregory Pardlo's collection *Digest* won the 2015 Pulitzer Prize for Poetry. Pardlo is also the author of *Air Traffic*, a memoir in essays, and *Totem*. His poems and essays have appeared in *The New Yorker*, *Playboy*, *American Poetry Review*, *Boston Review*, *The Nation*, *The New York Times* and elsewhere. His other honors include fellowships from the New York Public Library's Cullman Center, the Guggenheim Foundation, the New York Foundation for the Arts and the National Endowment for the Arts, among others. Pardlo is poetry editor at *Virginia Quarterly Review*, codirector of the Institute for the Study of Global Racial Justice at Rutgers University and a visiting associate professor of practice in Literature & Creative Writing at NYU Abu Dhabi.

A NOTE ON THE TYPE

This book was set in Janson, a typeface long thought to have been made by the Dutchman Anton Janson, who was a practicing typefounder in Leipzig during the years 1668–1687. However, it has been conclusively demonstrated that these types are actually the work of Nicholas Kis (1650–1702), a Hungarian, who most probably learned his trade from the master Dutch typefounder Dirk Voskens. The type is an excellent example of the influential and sturdy Dutch types that prevailed in England up to the time that William Caslon (1692–1766) developed his own incomparable designs from them.

Composed by North Market Street Graphics
Lancaster, Pennsylvania

Printed and bound by Friesens
Altona, Manitoba

Designed by Soonyoung Kwon